THE WEATHER REPORT

AIR PRESSURE DRIVING THE WEATHER!

EDITED BY JOANNE RANDOLPH

SUNDAY   MONDAY   TUESDAY   WEDNESDAY   THURSDAY   FRIDAY   SATURDAY

This edition published in 2018 by:
Enslow Publishing, LLC.
101 W. 23rd Street, Suite 240
New York, NY 10011

Cataloging-in-Publication Data

Names: Randolph, Joanne, editor.
Title: Air pressure driving the weather! / edited by Joanne Randolph.
Description: New York : Enslow Publishing, 2018 | Series: The weather report |
Includes bibliographical references and index. | Audience: Grades 3-5.
Identifiers: ISBN 9780766090071 (library bound) | ISBN 9780766090057 (pbk.) | ISBN 9780766090064 (6 pack)
Subjects: LCSH: Winds--Juvenile literature. | Winds--Speed--Measurement--Juvenile literature. | Atmospheric pressure--Juvenile literature.
Classification: LCC QC931.4 A57 2018 | DDC 551.51/8—dc23

Printed in the United States of America

To Our Readers: We have done our best to make sure all website addresses in this book were active and appropriate when we went to press. However, the author and the publisher have no control over and assume no liability for the material available on those websites or on any websites they may link to. Any comments or suggestions can be sent by email to customerservice@enslow.com.

Photo Credits: Cover, p. 1 Mark Schwettmann/Shutterstock.com (bridge), jassada watt/Shutterstock.com (clouds), solarseven/Shutterstock.com (weather symbols); series logo, NPeter/Shutterstock.com; interior pages background image, back cover, Sabphoto/Shutterstock.com; pp. 3, 28, 30, 32 Igor Zh./Shutterstock.com; pp. 4, 10, 14 bunnavit pangsuk/Shutterstock.com; p. 5 iofoto/Shutterstock.com; p. 6 Crystal-K/Shutterstock.com; p. 8 ottoflick/Shutterstock.com; p. 11 Image Source/Getty Images; p. 12 DemianM/Shutterstock.com; p. 13 Leonard the food guy/Shutterstock.com; pp. 15, 24 Jim Reed/Science Source/Getty Images; p. 16 Wichita Eagle/Tribune News Service/Getty Images; p. 18 Designua/Shutterstock.com; p. 19 Minerva Studio/Shutterstock.com; p. 21 Photo Researchers/Science Source/Getty Images; p. 23 RNGS/RTR/Newscom; p. 25 © AP Images; p. 26 flickr/NSSL NOAA/flickr.com/photos/47838549@N08/7468632490/CC BY-ND 2.0.

Article Credits: Stephen James O'Meara, "The Powers of Pressure," *Odyssey*; Nick D'Alto, "People to Discover: Meteorologist Ken Aucoin: 'Weighing In' on Atmospheric Pressure," *Odyssey*; Stephen James O'Meara, "The Kansas Killer!" *Odyssey*.

All articles © by Carus Publishing Company. Reproduced with permission.

CONTENTS

CHAPTER ONE

THE POWERS OF PRESSURE

F eeling pressured? Don't worry, so is everyone else across the globe. It's a fact. Each day, every day, all day, Earthlings wake up under pressure. What's more, for most of us, it's inescapable—even when we sleep. Of course, most of us wouldn't want it any other way, because without this kind of pressure—**air pressure**, that is—life, as we now enjoy it, simply wouldn't exist.

You don't feel it, but there is air pressure weighing down on you at all times.

Atmosphere of Earth

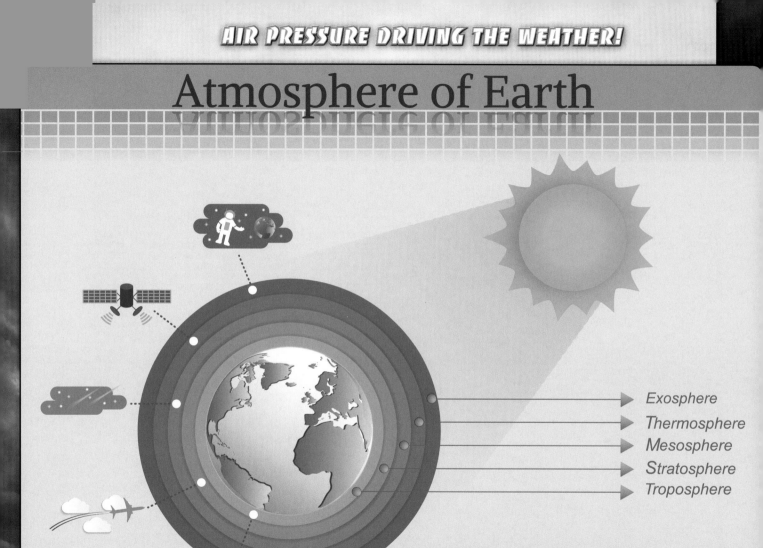

Exosphere

Thermosphere

Mesosphere

Stratosphere

Troposphere

This diagram shows the layers of Earth's atmosphere. The layers are different thicknesses, but from the top of the atmosphere to sea level is 500 miles (805 km), which is a little farther than driving from Boston to New York and back.

AIR PRESSURE ON EARTH

Ever feel like you're walking on air? Well, you do it every day. From the tip of your head to the bottom of your feet, air surrounds you. Air **molecules** are invisible, but they still have weight and take up space—and their weight is pressing against you. You're so used to this air pressure that you don't feel it.

If we could weigh a column of air one inch square that extended all the way to the "top" of the **atmosphere** (about 500 miles or 805 kilometers), it would weigh approximately 14.7 pounds at **sea level**. Thus, atmospheric pressure at sea level is approximately 14.7 pounds per square inch (psi), which equals one atmosphere. (A column of air measuring one square centimeter would weight about one kilogram). Pressure does not stop at sea level. It increases as depth below sea level increases. (The opposite, of course, happens when you climb in **altitude**—by approximately 1.0 psi for every 2,343 feet or 714 meters.)

Meteorologists use an instrument called a barometer to measure air pressure. Invented by Italian physicist Evangelista Torricelli in 1643, the first barometer was a glass tube with mercury inside that would rise and fall with the air pressure. Today, scientists use digital barometers.

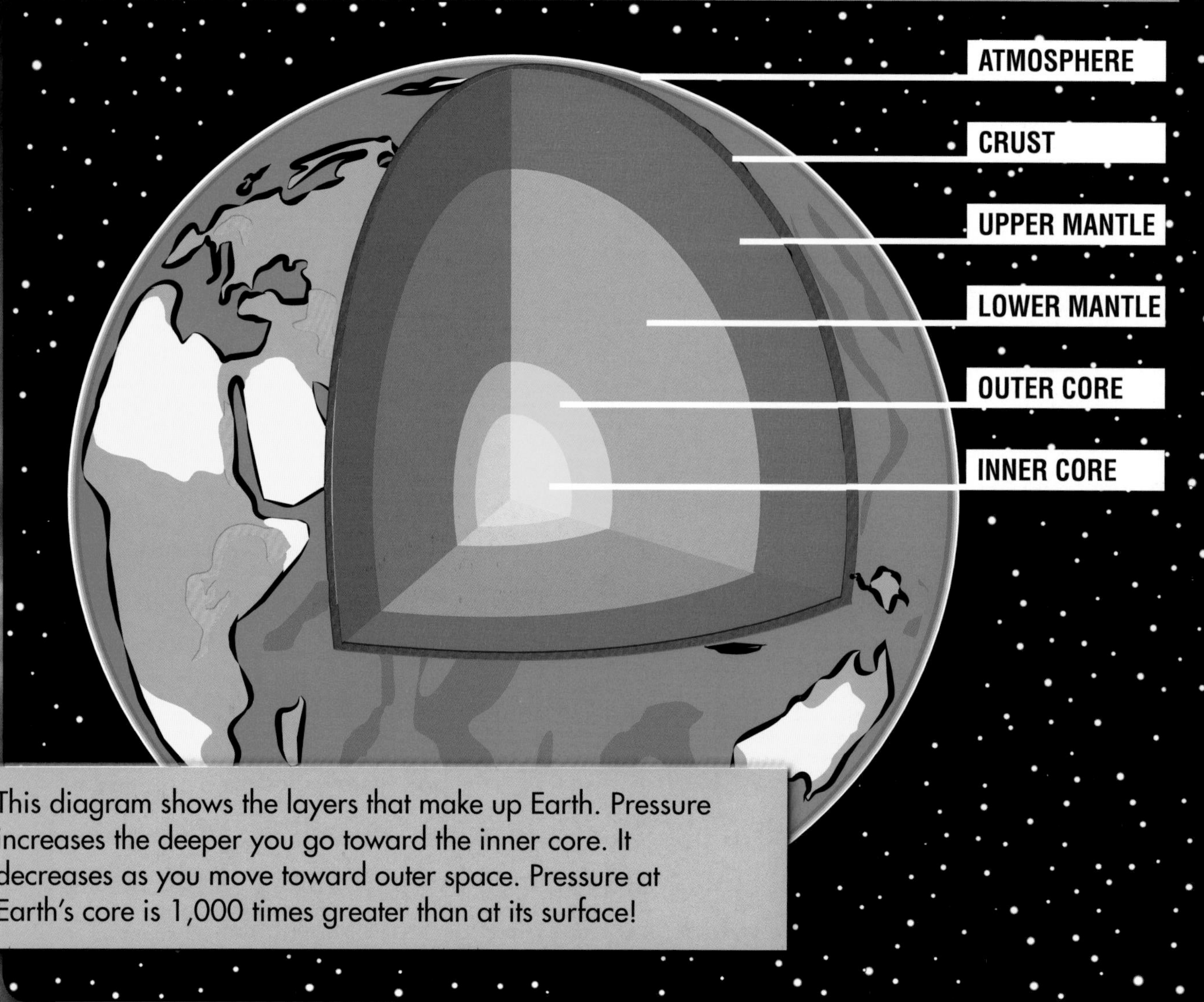

ATMOSPHERE

CRUST

UPPER MANTLE

LOWER MANTLE

OUTER CORE

INNER CORE

This diagram shows the layers that make up Earth. Pressure increases the deeper you go toward the inner core. It decreases as you move toward outer space. Pressure at Earth's core is 1,000 times greater than at its surface!

PRESSURE INSIDE EARTH

The pressure inside Earth is tremendous—so tremendous that we have to leave behind human experience and try to picture the forces with our imaginations. Consider, for instance, that oxygen—a simple, colorless, odorless gas at sea level—would **crystallize** under a pressure of 55,000 atmospheres! If you could **descend** about 2 miles (3 km) toward the geometrical center of Earth, you would feel a thousand times more pressure on you than you would at sea level. If you could journey about 3,700 miles (5,955 km) to the very **core** of Earth, you'd experience a pressure of some 3.5 million atmospheres! You wouldn't have to worry about gym class anymore because even the thought of doing a sit-up under these conditions would be painfully impossible.

The pressure on and inside Earth doesn't hold a candle to the stars and black holes and other space stuff, but that's a topic for another book! Just remember, the next time you stumble out of bed and feel so heavy that you can hardly shuffle your feet across the floor, just be thankful that your floor is on the surface of Earth and not inside it or in outer space!

CHAPTER TWO

"WEIGHING IN" ON ATMOSPHERIC PRESSURE

You may be wondering what air pressure has to do with the weather. You've seen those TV weather maps. They have lots of "high pressure" and "low pressure" zones. So how exactly does pressure translate into sunny days—or rained-out ballgames? It's simple. Atmospheric pressure happens because the air has weight. Weather happens because the weight of that air changes over a given area.

As temperature of air changes, it impacts the weight. Colder air is heavier than warmer air. Heavier air sinks, which makes atmospheric pressure over that area higher, producing few clouds—and terrific weather. (You'll see a big "H" on a TV weather map.)

All the Ls and Hs on this weather map denote high and low pressure areas.

Temperatures tend to stay the same during the day and night when it's cloudy. The clouds act like a blanket keeping the heat from escaping into the upper atmosphere.

Lighter, warmer air rises, making way for cooler air beneath. That makes atmospheric pressure lower (marked by an "L" on the weather map). Now clouds can form. Why? Because air that rises at a region of low pressure is moist with water that **condenses** at higher (colder) altitudes. Storms often follow.

Here's another way to think about how pressure impacts weather. It is kind of like shaking up a can of soda. The pressure in the can increases as you shake it. When you open the top, the soda sprays out of the can. It does this because you've created a difference in pressure. The high pressure inside the can rushes into the lower pressure air outside of the can. In the atmosphere, that kind of pressure difference creates wind.

Hurricanes are rated from 1 to 5 based on the speed of their winds. A Category 1 is the weakest, while a Category 5 has winds greater than 157 miles (252 km) per hour.

Winds always blow from areas of high pressure into areas of low pressure. If the pressure difference (or "**pressure gradient**") is small, you might detect a gentle breeze. But if the pressure difference is large (a big difference in pressure over a short distance), that can generate a huge wind—the kind you would experience during a hurricane or tornado.

13

CHAPTER THREE

THE KANSAS KILLER!

Keeping track of air pressure is important to meteorologists who work to predict the weather. They especially want to predict dangerous, extreme weather such as tornadoes and hurricanes. Let's take a look at one such storm and find out why it is so important for people to have some warning before extreme weather hits.

A massive, wedge-shaped tornado descended on Greensburg, Kansas, like an ax. Most twisters are only a few hundred yards across and remain on the ground for a few miles. But the Kansas Killer was monstrously different. When it struck on the evening of May 4, 2007, the violently rotating column of air measured almost 2 miles (about 3 km) across,

Meteorologists use satellite images and other weather data, including changes in air pressure, to track and predict storms.

packed winds in excess of 205 miles (330 km) per hour and remained on the ground for perhaps 100 miles (161 km) at a stretch.

The next morning, survivors faced reality—95 percent of their town was gone.

The Kansas Killer was one of several twisters that touched down that night in May. These tornadoes were part of a larger superstorm that produced seventy-two known tornadoes in forty-eight hours!

15

The rapidly rotating winds create an intense low pressure area inside the funnel.

WHAT IS A TORNADO?

A tornado is a violently whirling column of wind extending from the ground to a thundercloud's base. This column of air forms when a wall of warm, moist air meets a wall of cool, dry air. These air masses collide, moving the warm air up and the cool air under. The warm air updrafts can blow faster than 100 miles (161 km) per hour, launching the warm, moist air far up into the sky before it hits a cooler current of air called a **jet stream**.

The Greensburg twister began forming after 5 p.m. when a low-pressure area from the west encountered a warm front moving over the Texas Panhandle. Fed by moisture from the Gulf of Mexico and dry air flowing east from the southwest deserts, this collision formed a **supercell**, which leads to severe weather such as high winds, lightning, thunder, heavy rains, and maybe even hail, when moisture freezes in the upper atmosphere). The circular motion in a supercell is called a **mesocyclone**. When the mesocyclone is detected by radars, the National Weather Service (NWS) sends out a tornado warning, letting people know that tornadoes could form and/or one has been seen on the ground.

Clouds swirling with rotating funnel clouds hanging down mean a tornado could form at any second. Winds blowing in opposite directions

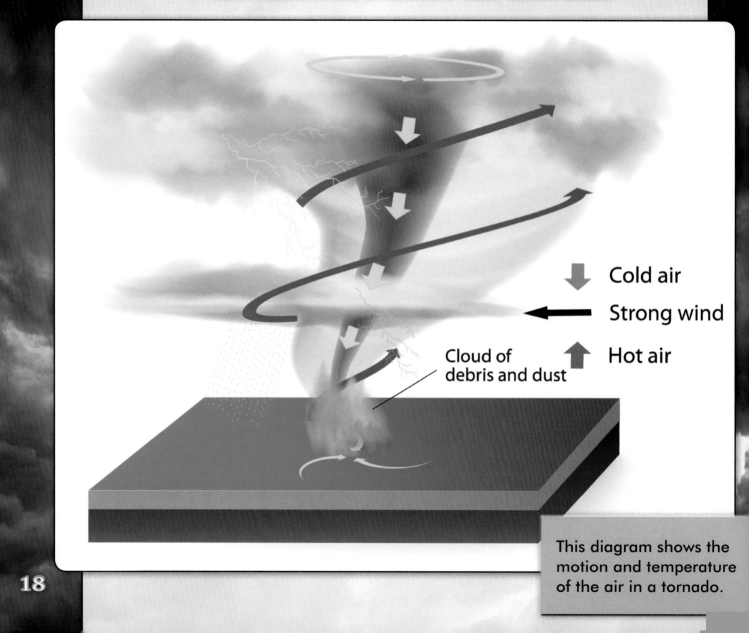

Cold air

Strong wind

Hot air

Cloud of
debris and dust

This diagram shows the
motion and temperature
of the air in a tornado.

A supercell storm can be a dramatic sight and it often brings dramatic weather, too! A supercell is basically a thunderstorm that forms from a mesocyclone, or a body of rotating air with a big updraft.

around a strong updraft start a narrow, violent whirl. **Centrifugal** forces push the air away from the center, leaving a low-pressure core that acts like a powerful **vacuum**.

A strong whirlwind of dust might be the first sign of a tornado. At the same time, a short funnel may form from the storm cloud above it. When the funnel connects with the rotating column on the ground, a tornado is created.

19

STORM WARNINGS

The Kansas Killer claimed ten lives in Greensburg and two outside town. But it could have been worse without National Oceanic and Atmospheric Administration (NOAA) warnings.

As early as 3 p.m., Kansas weather forecasters alerted residents in and around Greensburg to expect major storm activity. The first tornado warning was issued at 8:35 p.m. An hour later, several storm chasers saw the funnel cloud—a massive wedge that expanded to half a mile (a little less than one kilometer) in diameter in minutes—touch down southwest of Greensburg.

The funnel cloud descended 300 yards (274 meters) in front of storm chaser Dick McGown, then skipped across the ground for a few minutes before "establishing itself as a stout stovepipe." The tornado grew in size and strength as it headed for Greensburg. NOAA forecasters in Dodge City sent out a tornado warning thirty-nine minutes before the funnel hit town. Half an hour later, they issued a tornado emergency, the highest alert for extremely life-threatening situations, which urges residents to find shelter immediately.

Professional storm chasers watch for signs of tornadoes and then follow them to gather data or take photographs.

A Rare Breed

As the giant wedge approached Greensburg, several other **vortices** danced around it, according to McGown. It's possible that multiple tornadoes were on the ground at the same time farther north along the storm's track.

The low-pressure system that produced the Greensburg twister continued creating tornadoes for four hours. The next morning, twenty additional tornadoes' tracks were discovered in Greensburg and six neighboring counties. However, well-constructed structures were not damaged in these counties, where the tornadoes were rated class 0 or 1 on the Enhanced Fujita scale, a set of wind estimates (not measurements) based on damage, with 0 being the least damaging and 5 being the most.

The Greensburg twister was the first class 5 tornado to occur in the United States since the Enhanced Fujita scale was implemented on Feb. 1, 2007. It was also the largest tornado in the United States since May 3, 1999, when another devastating tornado killed thirty-six people and caused more than one billion dollars in damage as it ripped through Moore, Oklahoma. The Kansas Killer belongs to a rare breed of twisted destroyers; class 5 tornadoes form only once every few years in the United States.

Enhanced Fujita scale for tornadoes

Introduced in 1971 and updated in 2007, the Enhanced Fujita scale (EF scale) rates the strength of tornadoes in the U.S. and Canada based on the damage they cause.

Estimated wind speed (mph)

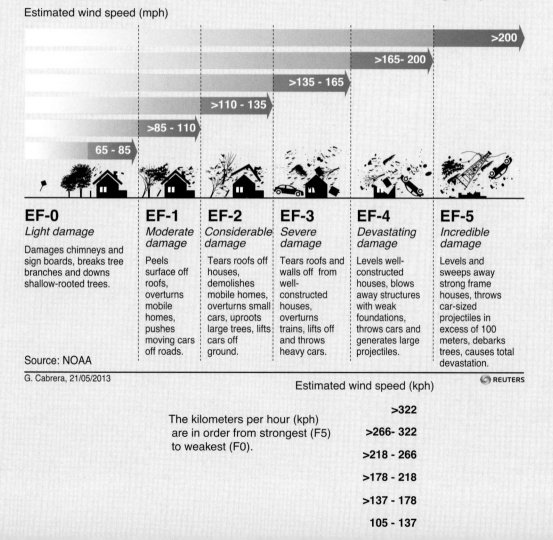

>200

>165- 200

>135 - 165

>110 - 135

>85 - 110

65 - 85

EF-0
Light damage

Damages chimneys and sign boards, breaks tree branches and downs shallow-rooted trees.

EF-1
Moderate damage

Peels surface off roofs, overturns mobile homes, pushes moving cars off roads.

EF-2
Considerable damage

Tears roofs off houses, demolishes mobile homes, overturns small cars, uproots large trees, lifts cars off ground.

EF-3
Severe damage

Tears roofs and walls off from well-constructed houses, overturns trains, lifts off and throws heavy cars.

EF-4
Devastating damage

Levels well-constructed houses, blows away structures with weak foundations, throws cars and generates large projectiles.

EF-5
Incredible damage

Levels and sweeps away strong frame houses, throws car-sized projectiles in excess of 100 meters, debarks trees, causes total devastation.

Source: NOAA

G. Cabrera, 21/05/2013

REUTERS

Estimated wind speed (kph)

The kilometers per hour (kph) are in order from strongest (F5) to weakest (F0).

>322

>266- 322

>218 - 266

>178 - 218

>137 - 178

105 - 137

A Greensburg resident sits outside the storm cellar she hid in while the class 5 tornado tore through her community. Tornadoes do a lot of damage, but with enough warning, people can take shelter from a storm so they remain safe.

BLOWN AWAY

This twisted storm devastated Greensburg. In the 1,800-resident town, more than 960 homes were flattened or blown away. The hospital was badly damaged. More than 135 businesses sustained major damage, and the water tower was destroyed. But nothing compares to the twelve lives lost on the darkest night of Greensburg's history.

This aerial view of Greensburg after the tornado struck shows the incredible damage the storm caused. Most of the town was destroyed.

NOAA uses a radar that can scan the sky for severe storms in under a minute. It collects data on developing tornadoes in supercells.

According to NOAA, tornadoes are one of nature's most violent storms, resulting in eighty deaths and more than 1,500 injuries each year. Tornadoes come in all shapes and sizes and can occur in any state at any time of the year. In Southern states, tornado season is March through May. For Northern states, it's the summer. Roughly one thousand tornadoes rip through our country every year.

NOAA issues more than fifteen thousand severe storm and tornado watches and warnings each year. Training and technological advances in tornado **forecasting** have increased average lead time for warnings from six to eleven minutes, allowing people to be better prepared.

Remember, though, the most sophisticated technologies are worth little if people don't heed the warnings and prepare themselves.

GLOSSARY

air pressure The pressure placed on Earth by the weight of the air.

altitude The height of something, such as a mountain, from the ground or sea level.

atmosphere The blanket of gases surrounding a planet.

centrifugal Moving outward from the center.

condense To change from a gas to a liquid.

core The center.

crystallize To form crystals.

descend To go downward.

forecasting Predicting something based on past trends and patterns.

jet stream A band of westerly flowing air currents that travel around Earth several miles up in the atmosphere.

mesocyclone A whirling mass of air that can form in a supercell; its presence is a condition for a tornado warning.

meteorologist A person who studies weather.

molecule The smallest unit of a chemical substance.

pressure gradient The different between the high pressure system and the low pressure system in an area.

sea level An average level of the sea's surface that is used to measure geographical features on land.

supercell A system that creates severe thunderstorms and has rotating winds and strong updrafts that may produce hail or tornadoes.

vacuum A space without matter.

vortex (vortices) A spiraling mass of air (or water) that sucks everything toward its center.

FURTHER READING

Books

Chambers, Catherine. *Stickmen's Guide to Earth's Atmosphere in Layers.* Minneapolis, MN: Hungry Tomato, 2016.

Paris, Stephanie. *Pop! Air and Water Pressure.* New York, NY: Time for Kids, 2013.

Roker, Al. *Al Roker's Extreme Weather.* New York, NY: HarperCollins, 2017.

Seymour, Simon. *Tornadoes.* New York, NY: HarperCollins, 2017.

Thomas, Isabel. *Wind: Explore, Create and Investigate.* London, UK: QED Publishing, 2016.

WEBSITES

KidsGeo.com
www.kidsgeo.com/geography-for-kids/0049-atmospheric-pressure.php
Dive deeper into the topic of atmospheric pressure.

Science Kids, Wind Facts
www.sciencekids.co.nz/sciencefacts/weather/wind.html
Read more information about wind.

University of Illinois, Tree House Weather Kids
extension.illinois.edu/treehouse/airpressure.cfm?Slide=1
Learn more facts about air pressure.

INDEX